TREASURES OF ANCIENT MEXICO
From the National Anthropological Museum

TEXT: MARIA ANTONIETA CERVANTES

Rights of total or partial reproduction and translation reserved.
World copyright of this edition:
©GEOCOLOR, S.A. ®

Travesera de Gracia, 15 - Barcelona (21) - Spain
2nd. Edition, March 1978
I.S.B.N.
84-7424-002-6

Library of Congress Catalog Card Number: 78-53024
All rights reserved.
This edition is published by Crescent Books, a division of
Crown Publishers, Inc.

a b c d e f g h

CRESCENT BOOKS
New York

We have much pleasure in thanking the Secretariat of Public Education and the Institute of History and Anthropology for their generous assistance in the compiling of this book which we dedicate to Mexico.

JUAN GRIJALBO

President of Geocolor, S. A.

(1) This statue of the rain god, Tlaloc, is from Coatlinchán. It belongs to the Teotihuacán culture, to the classical period dating between 400 and 600 A.D.

MUSEO NACIONAL DE ANTROPOLOGIA

(2) (3) (4) Different architectural views of the museum.

(5) Coatlicue, the mother god of the Mexicas. ▷

INTRODUCTION. The Museum

A museum is a permanent public institution which keeps and makes the cultural possessions of a nation known. Furthermore, it responds to a social need for information and is a means through which the concepts and ideas of the group it represents are communicated.

As a general rule, museums represent the greatest cultural achievements of peoples, and they appreciate objects as artistic attainments, emphasizing only their aesthetic value and not seeing them merely as a product of a social context.

We consider that museums along with popular literature and the general news media should help to make knowledge widely available, and accessible to the vast general public.

THE NATIONAL ANTHROPOLOGICAL MUSEUM

The National Anthropological Museum aims to show the history of the prehispanic peoples who inhabited what is now the land of Mexico and the changes they underwent on making contact with the Europeans, also the present situation of native groups in the country.

(6) A portrayal of the moon, Coyolxauhqui in Nahuatl.

(7) A monument dedicated to the "Fifth sun" also known as the "Aztec calender". ▷

So as to make this information more available to the public and to make the whole situation of ancient and contemporary native societies more clearly and objectively understood, we have proposed a new outline of social development which aims to improve upon the partial view shown at present by the Anthropological Museum.

This study is composed of three parts: Prehispanic Archaeology, the European Conquest and Ethnography. The first section represents a very lengthy period of time and for this reason it has been divided up into three chapters based on the different levels of social complexity most characteristic of Mexico they are: 1) Hunters and Gatherers. 2) Farmers, and 3) The State.

The second part refers to the Spanish Conquest and to the changes it brought about in the villages of the area in question.

The third part is an ethnographic approach to the present day indigenous groups, emphasizing the survival of prehispanic and colonial cultural patterns. The analysis of

(8) A view of the Oaxaca Room.

(9) A view of the Maya room. (10) Mexican room.
(11) Toltec room. (12) Teotihuacán room. (13)
Mexican room. (14) Teotihuacan room.

these three societies will be made taking into account the following fundamentals:
A) The Economic process, composed of all the productive activities.
B) The Legislative-Political process, that is, the mecanism of public administration.
C) The Ideological process, as portrayed in religion, magic and in art.
Social changes are studied as an internal process of change represented by the evolution of production relations. Originally, these production relations came about between two groups of the same village who were distinguished from each other only because they carried out different productive activities, such as: hunting and gathering, which do not imply class differences. In a

superior stage of development it is possible to define the existence of an exploiting class above a productive class. Therefore, we have taken into consideration that the main role in social changes is played by the class struggle.
It must be clearly stated that we will treat the societies in the mesoamerican area (Map 1) as a whole, in which the groups existing there, such as the mayas, the teotihua-cans, the aztecs or mexicas, share, through the course of history, similar modes of social organization with a wide variety of formal expression; this variety can be seen in the language differences, in the mode of dress and orna-mentation, in architectural styles, and in crafts such as pottery, sculpture, weaving and painting.
And it is the study of this variety which is the most exci-ting aspect of the work of the anthropologist.

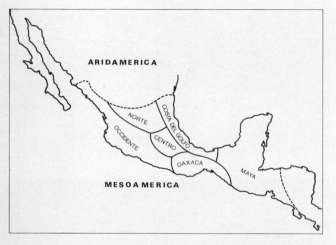

Map 1. The geographical area and internal division of the mesoamerican territory.

UNIT I. ARCHAEOLOGY
Chapter 1. Hunters and Gatherers

Some 30000 years ago, northern Asia was inhabited by hunters and nomadic gatherers who lived in organized bands or family groups. They hunted animals and gathered plants useful for food. This way of life necessitated the domination of a wide stretch of territory by the band, and thus they controlled a certain area and fought to defend it. As the number of bands increased, some ousted others who in their turn had to look for new territory. One of the results of this process of expansion was the population of the American continent by groups from Asia (Photo 15). The fact that at this time the two continents were connected by a spit of land now known as the Behring Strait also formed part of this process. This natural bridge existed at that time as it was a period of coldness on the earth and a great mass of frozen water had accumulated at the poles and in the mountains, the sea then being small with many free tracts of land now covered by water. All higher land, even small peaks, were snow covered and only the valleys were free of ice. The land was occupied by animals such as the mammoth, the bison, the ant-eating bear, the sabre-toothed tiger, the long-haired horse and others (Photo 16). Roots and plants grew in the valleys, these were mainly grassy in type and able to be used as food.

The population expanded throughout the whole American continent from Alaska to Patagonia, and at the end of the process the Antilles were populated.

The hunters and gatherers made tools with all the materials within their reach which were used as an extension of human strength, that is for use as levers. Using pressure and percussion, they made hand axes, chopping knives and sharp heads for projectiles for hunting and killing animals. Stone was used mainly, but there were also tools made out of wood and bone.

These stone tools for hunting have occasionally been found together with the skeletons of extinct species of animals in what are known as slaughtering areas. (Photos 17 and 19).

Baskets were used in the gathering of plants, nets for the transport of seeds such as amaranth and the sweet opuntia seed, and sets of tools made in stone for cutting and grinding the produce from the crop. The band of people was not stable in its composition and kept together or divided up according to the temporary activity they were devoted to in order to get food, as for example, hunting a large animal like the mammoth when the largest number of people possible was needed, led by one or by several persons. In these large animal hunts all members of the band took part, women and children helping in the less risky tasks such as driving the animals or helping in the making and positioning of traps. Work was divided up according to age and sex, but everyone worked together in the same activity. When hunting smaller animals a lesser number of members of the band took part and in general people of one sex or of a certain age, depending of course on the techniques used in the operation; for example, they formed lines of people to round up the animals until they were in a confined area when they were killed with clubs.

Another technique was to run the animals off the edge of a cliff — the animals were rounded up and driven to a ravine where they were killed on falling. For these groups of people fishing was an important productive activity, along with the gathering of sea fruits. Tools such as forks, hooks and harpoons were used for fishing, while in lakes and shallow rivers nets and fykes were used. The techniques were similar in this territory to those used in other parts of the world. The gathering of sea fruits was done by groups on the coasts, mainly those living in estuaries.

On the other hand, when the predominating productive activity of the band was picking plants, all members participated, again led by one or several organizers who were more adept and knowledgeable in these tasks. The produce of the harvest and the hunt was shared equally among all members of the band, although perhaps on occasion, the organizer of the hunt or the harvest took a better share of what was produced.

These occasional differences as regards the quality or the quantity of the shares did not basically change the organization or the predominating relationship between people. Furthermore, leadership in these activities was of a temporary nature, and constantly changing from one individual to another.

Another integrating element in the band were the kinship systems, which were the expression of the need for survival. In a group of hunters and gatherers everyone is realted, and further, if a person is not tied by a real or an imaginary relationship, he is considered an enemy; thus the necessary bonds were established to maintain the structure of the band. The elders, relying on their knowledge, directed the group in general matters, these constituted the moral authority and were the counsellors, but in some cases this authority could devolve upon the strongest, or the best hunter or reaper even if he were young. Up to now, few representative elements of the ideology of these groups have been found. The carved bone of Tequixquiac corresponds to this stage; it is a

(16) The animals found by the first hunters in America were the mammoth, the bison, the anteating bear, the sabre-toothed tigre, the camel, and the long-haired horse.

fossilized camel bone on which the figure of an animal has been worked (Photo 18).

In general, these objects, paintings and reliefs exalt hunting, portray some ancestor or tell of original myths. Through song, rites and dances, always related to basic group activities, these people reinforced their unity and succeeded in reproducing the same forms of life.

In these societies, as has already been stated, the leadership of the group was undertaken without any special distinction, by the best hunter or the best reaper, and when it was not a question of these activities, family bonds governed the destiny of the group. On occasion, the two fundamental activities and their organization when undertaken simultaneously gave rise to difficult decision making — either the hunt or the harvest — or even to problems between leaders.

Within this context, the general tendency was that the men who controlled the reaping tended to develop more effective techniques for harvesting for which more people were needed for a longer period of time, this tended to more intensive methods of reaping originating the domestication of certain plants together with a more sedentary and established way of life, all of which went against the nomadic existence so propitious to hunting which became a complementary activity and prevailed as a method of organization in case of war. Among the first products cultivated was maize (Photo 25) which began by being a very small wild plant with few rows of seeds; through cultivation it became the most effective basic food plant of the mesoamerican peoples up to the present time.

Within this same process, the gatherers built the first known villages in the mesoamerican territory, some 5 000 years ago. These were composed of a few houses, sometimes semi-subterranean, made of stone, wood, and palm leaves, situated near rivers or sources of water where it was very easy to obtain wild products from gathering, and to cultivate maize, marrows, kidney beans and chiles. They also continued to hunt animals and to fish.

This new sedentary way of life expressed itself in changes in the work tools, as they were now not only made of stone but out of clay (Photos 23 and 24) as it was necessary to store and cook the grain, there were also stones for grinding or metates and stone pots for

(17) *When they were able to kill a mammoth, they ate its flesh and used its hide for clothes, tools were made out of the bones.*

(18) *The hunters carved an animal on this camel bone.*

(19) *Tools such as these were used to hunt and quarter animals.*

(20) *Nets, baskets and decoration made out of vegetable fibres were used by groups of gatherers.*

(21) *The gatherers living in the north of mesoamerica buried their dead with vegetable fibre turbans and shell-shaped adornments.*

(22) *Groups living in the north of Mesoamerica developed harvesting until the arrival of the Spaniards.*

(23) *Clay and stone receptacles appeared when man began to cultivate the earth.*

(24) *One of the first vessels made by the farmers.*

(25) *Maize was the staple food of the prehispanic peoples. The cultivation of this plant was a long and important process.*

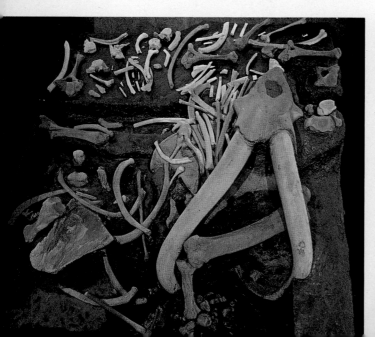

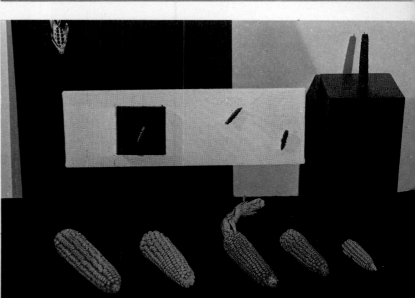

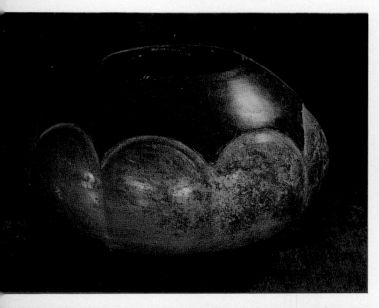

(26) The first vessels produced by agricultural societies were in imitation of simples shapes present in nature.

(27) Clay mask used in funeral rites.

(28) Occasionally they modelled their vessels in human shape to place them as offerings to the dead. This one is an acrobat from Tlatilco, Mexico.

preparing the food. They still carried on making baskets, matting, and several types of objects such as ornaments for the head and body made from vegetable fibres. The transformation of the groups of hunters and gatherers into the sedentary agricultural groups described earlier ocurred mainly in two areas of American territory: the Andes and Mesoamerica.

The groups inhabiting the rest of the continent continued to develop intensive plant gathering in semi-desert areas (Photo 21 and 22) and the gathering of sea fruits on the coast. Groups living in areas near the poles specialized in hunting; thus these groups continued, almost without change, until their contact with the Europeans in the XVI century, and much later than that in some cases.

Chapter 2. The Farmers

Between 2000 B.C. and the year 0, mesoamerican societies had reached the stage of social development known as village dwellers, based on an agricultural and sedentary life.

The main source of energy was still man, as in this territory there were no animals that could be used for work purposes.

The earth was worked using very simple production techniques: in order to prepare the earth they usually felled the trees and plants they found there, with polished stone axes, letting them dry and afterwards burning them. To plant maize seeds and other seeds for cultivation they only used a sharp pointed stick (the "coa").

To supplement their diet they hunted with the aid of traps, bows and arrows with obsidian or flint heads and wooden lances also with stone tips.

They fished in rivers and lakes with nets woven from vegetable fibres, lances and harpoons, and built canoes for transport. They also picked plants that grew wild, such as the Indian fig, amaranth, agave, certain grasses and tubers.

They used knives made of obsidian for their domestic work which were highly effective and obtained from a nucleus by means of a technique of preparation of this nucleus and percussion; they were quite fragile but were produced by the hundred. They used metates of basaltic stone with pestils to grind the maize and other seeds, also scrapers, choppers and a whole set of carved and polished stone instruments.

Their weaving was not developed, as a general rule people at this time went nude, wearing only cotton head-dresses, but the instruments for this craft have not been found. Some minerals were exploited such as vermilion which they used to decorate their bodies and faces with, for burying their dead, and as a decoration on certain ceremonial vessels. They mined pyrites, a mineral which when polished reflects images; this was used for mirrors; nephrite, amathyst and other stones were also found in the shape of adornments.

The village territory was communal property and as extensive as the cultivated lands necessary to satisfy the needs of the group as regards food.

The families lived in houses which as a whole made up the village, these houses were distributed round the most important buildings which were communal and almost always related with all the elements of organization and integration of the group, such as religious and administrative buildings, also places for exchange and redistribution.

For building houses, the most easily obtained local

(29) (30) Sorcerors played an important part in this society as they cured people and took part in the leadership of the group.

(31) The Olmecs lived on the gulf coast in centres like San Lorenzo, Ver. and La Venta, Tab. where sculptures of mythical beings like this jaguar man have been found.

(32) This sorcerer has covered himself with a tiger skin, probably to show the origin of his lineage.

materials were used, that is, wood and stone for the base, straw for the roof and sun dried brick for the walls. The largest buildings were initially mounds of earth which became transformed into stone pyramids holding up the temples; squares for meetings and public festivities were sometimes defined by stones in the shape of stockades; in some centres there were stone drains and large tombs where outstanding people in the community were buried. Each family worked on the communal land belonging to the village, every member of the family took part in these agricultural tasks at different times and for different activities, according to age and sex. One part of the harvest was kept for sowing next season, and finally another part which they had to produce over and above the quota was

(34) The Olmecs depicted themselves as tubby people with child-like faces and with the head out of proportion.

(35) They portrayed their chiefs in great sculpted stone heads thus lending importance to their villages.

kept for building and communal ritual. Also they had to work on the communal buildings which at this stage of their development were not made to increase production but simply to exalt group unity.

Due to the fact that farming activities occupied the workers for a short period per year, it was possible to develop crafts which were a complementary productive activity to agriculture. There were no people specialized in craft work.

Perhaps the most important of the crafts in this type of society was pottery (Photo 26) which was born from the need to store and cook food: later pottery was also made as something to be exchanged with other groups, or for rituals or as offerings to the dead (Photos 28 and 33). It is well known that each group developed different shapes of pottery with their own patterns. The patterns or styles did not easily change with time, which is why we can take them as terms of reference to identify the different groups inhabiting the mesoamerican area. The same thing occurs with the clay figures, each group developing techniques and styles different from the rest.

Their statues were modelled for ritual purposes but also represented different aspects of village life, for example, through them we are able to find out not only the physical aspect of each village, but some of their practices of adornment such as the deformation of the skull, head sha-

(33) Olmec ceramic vases with mythological designs on them were exchanged for other products such as obsidian and salt.

(36) These jade figures found in La Venta, Tab. probably represent a meeting of chiefs.

(39) God of fire appearing on the pyramid of Cuicuilco D.F.

ving, the custom of painting the face and the body (Photos 42 and 44) and the types of headdresses and ornaments they used.

On the coast of the Gulf of Mexico, the Olmecs developed the sculpture of stone and gem cutting (Photo 31). Both in their large sculptures as in their small clay and flint stone figures, they portrayed themselves as tubby and with child-like faces. (Photo 34). They were very able in working with precious stones. (Photo 36). They obtained nephrite, pyrate and amathyst by means of exchange with other groups in the Guerrero area.

Through this exchange they spread their art to other regions of mesoamerica where sculptures of this kind have been found.

Occasionally, villages belonged to larger units known as tribes, a good example of this were the Olmec centres

(37) This small ceremonial axe in green stone depicts a jaguar man.

(38) Jade figurines were used for exchange purposes between the Olmecs and other groups.

(40) This sculpture named "The wrestler" corresponds to the later years of the Olmec group.

(41) One of the first mesoamerican gods was the old god or the god of fire.

(42) Through their clay figures we are able to recognise the different types of adornment made by the prehispanic peoples, such as tattooing and deforming the head.

(43) Human head in central Veracruz style.

(44) There existed many different customs in the way of adorning the body and the head.

(45) The potters in every group in Mesoamerica made vessels in different ways.

(46) They represented scenes from everyday life in clay.

(47) Shell-work is a typical craft of the western region.

(48) The internal
relations of
the group were
sustained through
living together.

(49) Masculine figure with a pectoral decoration in the form of a tortoise-shell.

(50) Female figure from the west of Mexico.

such as San Lorenzo in Veracruz, La Venta in Tabasco and Tres Zapotes in Veracruz; these centres controlled the produce of several villages and re-distributed it, thus making a closed system.

The re-distribution centres marked their importance by decorating the place with large sculptures (Photo 35) mounds of earth, and in general more important communal undertakings than those existing in the remaining villages within the system.

The villages depending on the tribe were linked by a common ancestor or by lineage or alliances made for mutual protection against other villages or sometimes against societies of hunters and gatherers invading their territories. The villages were constantly at war, an activity in which all members cooperated according of course to age and sex.

Besides being an activity for defending or gaining territory, it was good for group unity and brought about a closer relationship between members of the village.

The leadership of the village rested with a group of individuals probably the elders, who had no real power but a temporal functional power; these were the ones who took decisions as to when they should sow the seed, about relations with other groups and who organized alliances with other villages through marriages, and who controlled the women, as these produced the work force; thus they maintained the same internal forms of group relationship. Sorcerers and incipient priests (Photos 29 and 30) were those charged with maintaining the internal ties of the group; they conserved the relationship with the tribe or larger unit which carried out redistribution, and had the control of medicine in their hands which was based on the administration of herbs and rites. (Photo 32).

These people maintained group unity through festivities, dances, chants and rites to the elements of nature which favoured the fertility of the earth.

The communal buildings and craft elements constituted a reinforcement of the values which the dominant group manipulated and which made up the established order. The body of leaders in the villages demanded more and more from its members in communal work and craft products to be used for exchanges with other villages, this led

(51) (52) Portrayals of family scenes are often found in the western region of México.

(53) The dog called "Izcuintle" was used as food and also as company by the mesoamerican groups.

(54) Elements of nature are reproduced in their ceramic art.

(55) This shell-mask was used to cover the face of a corpse.

to conflicts between the villages and for this reason it became necessary to designate a group of warriors to defend the riches accumulated in the centres which were in the hands of the leaders.

Communal work was still directed towards the construction of great buildings such as pyramids for temples, among them is the one at Cuicuilco dedicated to the god of Fire (Photo 41), these buildings consolidated the position of the group leaders even more.

This process created a climate of instability inside and outside the village, and this social tension was eventually resolved in fights between villages and also inside them. The best solution in such a state of tension was to form larger groups, and this was done through the unification of several villages which also gave rise to the first large scale division of labour and therefore the creation of social classes: the peasants or exploited class and the exploiters or leaders.

As there existed a union of villages as part of a greater unit, and on the other hand, a series of peasant communities, the organization did not now function with elders and sorcerers, and it was necessary for there to be an uprising of a group to take power, and with this to make decisions on internal relations and relations with other groups, the group in power would take advantage of the extra produce given by the villages in order to devote itself not to directly productive activities, but instead to those of leadership, using above all ideology as a controlling element.

This transformation ocurred in pre-hispanic Mexico some years before the Christian era.

Changes to this type of class ridden society where there existed larger units occured in some regions in the territory where a series of social factors came together and favoured the changes, but in some areas such as western Mexico or the so-called marginal area between mesoamerica and aridamerica, the situation did not change, instead the same ways of village level life were maintained for a long period of time, and the phenomenon of change did not take place until the XIII century; in other cases the situation did not change until the arrival of the Europeans. In the west of Mexico the village level life prevailed which is reflected in its clay artisanry depicting scenes from every day life (Photo 46), family life, (Photos 51 and 52) or family reunions or a meeting of the group controlling the villages. (Photo 48). They modelled vessels in vegetable, animal and human shapes (Photos 45, 53, 54, 56, 57, 58).

Chapter 3. The State

The population of various villages concentrated in new centres where the necessary buildings were made for the group's economic, political and religious activities. These centres quite often became actual cities.

As a result of this joining of various villages the first great division of labour was established between the urban centres or cities on the one hand, and the agricultural villages or the countryside on the other. Formerly the villages were composed according to an ethnic criterion, but this changed with the new order in which the ethnic element was overcome and the groups became integrated as a class, that is, according to the role they played in production, and not according to kinship or ethnic connection.

The disintegration of village societies and the existence of classes in relation to production led inexorably to the formation of state governed societies.

The state apparatus arose as the only possible satisfaction or palliative when there was a need to conciliate the different class interests of which the community was composed.

The state, as a conciliator, required power which was at the same time used to impose and perpetuate the condition of those who were exploited, to subjugate a class, or other surrounding communities. The state, in the beginning, only occupied itself with forcing the population to work more extensively, and had no interest in increasing the productive techniques of the villages under its rule; however only in the villages near to the city where the seat of government was situated and in the city itself was it possible to observe differences as in these places works of irrigation and communication were undertaken to improve production although they still continued to use stubbing and humid soil techniques and terracing on the hillsides. One of the innovations was the use of floating gardens *(chinampas)* in the lakeland areas; these consisted in marking off a portion of the lake with stakes and filling this part in with earth and mud from the lake itself until it reached a higher level than the surface of the lake, in this way there was always sufficient moisture for the crops.

As for work undertaken by the state, both the hydraulic and agricultural tasks which the peasants themselves had to work on were not of any great importance and consisted merely of dams to contain the water, constructions to divert the course of rivers and irrigate certain areas, and canals to bring water. There has been little evidence of these systems found by archaeologists.

The whole social organization became centralized in the city which was a centre with a considerable number and density of inhabitants where the elements of economic, political and religious control were to be found: there were public buildings such as pyramids, palaces, and administration buildings distributed around squares and along the streets. These buildings reflected both the internal and external organization of the State.

(56) Music played an important part in the life of these people.

The houses belonging to the ruling class were built near to the central religious administrative area; they were spacious, made of stone, and decorated with mural paintings.

Merchants also lived in the city who belonged to the ruling class that exchanged products with other villages and the larger unit, specialized craftsmen living in the centre were organized and their production controlled to satisfy the needs of the controlling group, the houses belonging to the craftsmen were distributed in districts

established according to family or ancestral links as previously, but according to social class, with the exception of the ruling group which was organized on the basis of family kinship.

Ownership of the land was still communal, but now administered by the state who established rules for its use and occasionally for the use of water sources, and these were distributed according to its convenience. The larger unit assigned certain lands to the control centres, these in their turn to the villages under their domination, and the village authorities assigned the land to each peasant family who worked on it. In order to handle the produce, the State maintained a series of smaller centres responsible for exchanging the excess produce from the villages for craft products or agricultural produce which was sent to the city or to the larger unit. The peasants also contri-

(58) In Jalisco they represented the common people in simple attitudes.

(57) In the region of Nayarit they had a very peculiar way of painting their head and body using nose and earings with many hoops.

according to their activity or depending on the region from which they came, as for example, in the Oaxacan district in Teotihuacan.

A large proportion of the population of the large centres or cities came from other parts of mesoamerica. The peasants did not live in the central part of the urban area, but occupied the surrounding villages and produced the food necessary to maintain the urban population.

The territory of this new social organization took in that of all the villages under its control, and the relationship between the villages and the larger unit was not

(59) The change which the rise of the Teotihuacán state brought about was reflected in all types of cultural expression.

(60) The different attitudes of this articulated doll and its movements allow ideas to be transmitted.

(61) These figurines called "retrato" are typical of Teotihuacán.

buted with manual labour and they were sent on to the larger unit when architectural or infrastructural work was to be undertaken. The control units, on the other hand, only received a series of superstructural elements from the centre, such as architectural plans, a certain shape or design of pottery, religious ideas and objects related to worship, but never food produce. The degree of relationship, or the importance of the control units could be measured by the quantity and quality of these elements, that is, the greater the quantity and quality, or the greater the similarity to objects and ideas in the centre, the more important the relationship. The more distant centres had fewer elements similar to those in the larger centre.

The relationship between the larger unit and the villages was brought about through the payment of tribute which was a tax imposed by the State on all groups under its control.

This tribute could be in the form of: forced labour for communal tasks; food products such as maize, kidney beans, grain and seeds; local products such as obsidian, salt, cotton, and honey; or raw materials changed into craft products such as cloth, embroidery, jewellery etc. The majority of the villages were self sufficient, but they had to produce more in order to pay the tribute; if they rebelled against this, the warriors of the larger unit declared war upon them, subjected the village to their authority once more and increased the amount of tribute to be paid. The villages were subjected either by voluntary alliances or by wars. So that this system could work, the participation of a well organized body of warriors was necessary; this fulfilled three main functions: it enlarged the territory by conquering more villages and these were exploited for more tribute; it controlled the area under its domination and protected the city and all dependent territory from invasions and wars with other groups. Military garrisons were maintained at specific points to control certain areas and to protect the production control centres.

There existed various levels of social differences established by the unequal sharing of wealth; firstly between the city or larger unit and the villages depending on it; and in second place between the ruling groups, craftsmen and peasants, both between those of the larger group and those of the control centres.

The craft and building work was carried out as an extra activity by the peasants of the agricultural villages who paid their tribute in this way to the ruling group.

Only sumptuary craft work such as embroidered blankets, crockery, jewellery and decorations were made by specialized artisans who lived in the cities. The production of these craft articles depended upon the needs of the ruling class, they lived in districts under the direct control of the rulers, and also painted and sculpted religious images.

The larger unit was constantly on the increase, people arrived at the city from other parts and settled in its confines as these larger centres constituted a special attraction.

The city increased considerably and more and more buildings were constructed, more civic buildings and especially religious buildings as these were one of the most effective means of control.

Ideology was expressed through art, religious concepts, and the general philosophy of the ruling class.

At this stage of development, ideology was completely directed towards the perpetuation of the system, mainly through increased knowledge and art.

Art served to distinguish the class in power, they were outstanding and portrayed themselves as god-sent. The ruling class favoured knowledge in order to have more possibilities of control in all areas.

The characteristics described were those present in prehispanic societies from the beginning of the Christian era till the arrival of the Spaniards. The main differences were to be seen in the superstructure temporally, and in material demonstrations geographically. Temporally, we can differentiate three stages in the development of State societies: the Theocratic State occuring between the years 0 and 900 A.D., the Military State from 900 to 1521, and a third stage including the change from one type of state to another. The production relationships prevailed and essentially the control elements of the ruling class were those that changed.

The main difference in material expression occured between the plateau societies and those of the low lands or tropic zones. The plateau area comprised the teotihuacan society, the Oaxaca, the Aztec, and those of the centre of .Veracruz. In the Low Lands the maya culture developed widely in what are now the states of Tabasco, Chiapas, Yucatán, Quintana Roo, and the Republics of El Salvador, Guatemala and Honduras.

Teotihuacán

In the centre of Mexico, this transformation of agricultural societies into state societies came about before it did in any other part of mesoamerica. This represented a noteworthy change in all cultural expression and social manifestations (Photo 59). One of the most significant elements in this new organization was the city; the seat of the teotihuacan state was in the city of the same name. The word Teotihuacán means "place of the gods" in nahuatl, the language spoken by the Aztecs in the XVI century. The names we use to describe the city, its temples and gods, all belong to the nahuatl language of the Aztecs who considered Teotihuacán a holy place. We do not know the name they applied to themselves nor the language they spoke at the time of their development.

(65) The craftsmen who made luxury
objects did so according to patterns
imposed on them by the ruling
class.

(66) (67) This frescoe painted vessel depicts
Tlaloc the god of rain.

(68) The Teotihuacans continued to worship the old god or the god of fire.

The city was the control centre of the area dominated by the State, there, there were mainly religious buildings, administrative buildings and the palaces of the rulers spaced out in areas nearest to the religious centre; father away were the houses of the traders and craftsmen; there were no peasants in this city.

The urban area had been carefully planned on two axes, the first from north to south (15° 30' east from astronomic north) this axis was a great avenue called calle de los Muertos (street of the Dead) along which were the main temples such as those of the Sun and Moon and those of Tláloc, los Subterráneos, and many others. The other axis ran from east to west and at the cross roads was the administrative area, that is, an area of public buildings, the market, and a construction known as the Citadel.

The city was divided off into squares from these two axes and everything was organized on this network basis.

The area of the city during the period of its greatest splendour was approximately 22sq. kms. and the population calculated to be between 75 000 and 200 000 inhabitants; it was situated in an open valley but with defensive elements, sometimes using barriers of cacti, and walled in other parts (5 kms. in length); other sections gave onto the cultivated area of Chinampas where the territory bordered lake Texcoco. The ceremonial area was an impressive ensemble of temples harmoniously set in large squares where the people gathered for ceremonies. The largest of these was dedicated to the goddess Chalchiuhtlicue, goddess of Sweet Waters; the remaining temples were dedicated to gods responsible for fertility and agriculture, there were no Sun gods of gods of Death in this type of theocratic society.

Very close to the ceremonial area were the palaces where the rulers and priests lived, these were well built stone constructions with flat roofs held up by pillars. The rooms were distributed around a central courtyard in the middle of which was a shrine. The walls of these palaces were decorated with pictures representing religious scenes. One of the most famous palaces is the so called Quetzal-papalotl or the Quetzal-Butterfly, as the latter are the most outstanding decorative motif.

Outside the areas where the rulers lived, the city was organized by districts, and in these people lived in a sort of multifamiliar apartment or apartments for many families where craftsmen devoted to the same task met together, for example craftsmen working in obsidian grouped together for making tools such as knives, or figures, which they exchanged in the market.

In excavations on the city, there appeared more than 500 workshops specializing in obsidian, this therefore must have been a very important industry. In other similar apartments lived craftsmen who worked in pottery, statuettes, gem-stones, shells and who cut metate and basalt mortars etc.

In the middle of each residential unit there were one or two small temples dedicated to the god who was the patron of these craftsmen.

Other districts were inhabited by the families of merchants where objects from Veracruz and maya areas, together with teotihuacan elements have been discovered; teotihuacan objects have also appeared in a great many mesoamerican regions, in far distant areas such as the coast of Chiapas, Kaminaljuyú and Tikal in Guatemala. Teotihuacan was a cosmopolitan centre, its population did not belong to one ethnic group, there were groups of families from other parts of mesoamerica for example, one district was occupied by people from Oaxaca, the greater part of the material found in excavations in this area was typical of that region and they even found a tomb in evident zapotec style.

All the information we possess regarding the development of Teotihuacán indicates that this city had an enormous attraction for different groups of people, even for those living far away, it was really the most important

(69) Orange coloured anthropomorphic vessel from the Teotihuacán period.

(70) This sculpture in the shape of a macaw head formed part of the building for the pelota game in Xochicalco, Morelos.

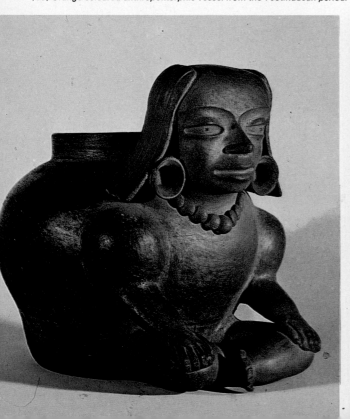

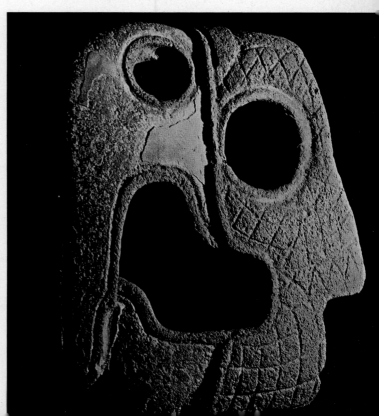

(71) The rulers of
the Teotihuacán state
created gods related to
agriculture, water, and
vegetation; this was
the goddess
Chalchiuhtlicue, lady of
the waters.

(72) *Mode of dress, decoration, and the practice of deforming the head and the teeth were related to social status.*

(73) *Ceramic ware from the gulf coast is characterized by the fine clay used to make it and the high quality of the design.*

(74) (75) (76) *Images of the yokes, palms and axes used by the pelota players. In this ceremony the loser was decapitated and he was buried with these stone objects.*

(77) *During the festivities to the god Xipe, the priest dressed in the skin of a victim.*

(78) *A common element in all the mesoamerican peoples was the god of rain, the one showing on this page is from the gulf coast.*

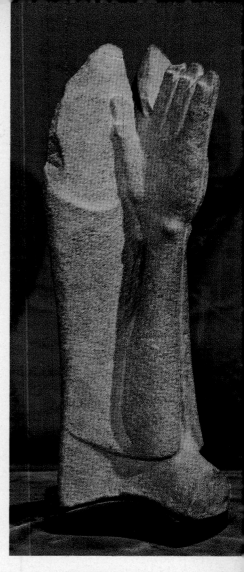

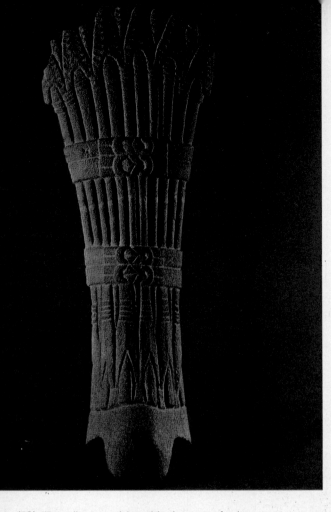

(79) "Palma" ceremonial used in the game of pelota.
(80) Vessel typical of the central area of Veracruz.
(81) Xochipilli was the god of flowers and song.

economic, religious and political centre in all mesoamerica which all merchants and craftsmen wanted to reach.

The architecture developed in the city represented and dignified the ruling group, it was massive and decorated with leaning sculptures, all of them painted; the masons and craftsmen working on it were the peasants who had to give manual labour besides a portion of their agricultural produce to maintain that over populated centre which did not produce food. They did not understand the symbolism their work represented as these were complicated ideological concepts handled only by the rulers. All crafts enjoyed an exceptional popularity, but there were few works of sculpture in statuary and these were of poor quality as not much importance was given to this branch of art; among these statues is Tlaloc situated at the entrance to the museum (frontispiece) and the goddess Chalchiuhtlicue who appeared on the so-called pyramid of the moon (Photo 71).

The potters, like all the other craftsmen, worked off models imposed on them by the ruling class, in their vessels and statuettes they portrayed religious concepts

(82) (83) *The god of death lived in the world of the shadows under the world of the living.*

(84) *Sculpture was used to transmit ideological and political concepts among the Maya people as among the rest of the mesoamerican peoples.*

(Photos 60 and 61) or made luxurious objects which constituted the household furniture of those of the higher class (Photo 64) and which occasionally served as offerings on the death of these personages (Photos 62 and 63).

The role of priests in this society was to reinforce the predominating system, creating more gods (Photos 66, 67, 68, 71) inventing myths, justifying the inequality between the classes and demanding tribute and labour. The priests also controlled mathematical knowledge, also knowledge of astronomy, the calender, and medicine etc., but as there are no documents refering to this period, we are unable to state anything further regarding them.

El Tajín

The city of El Tajín is the best example of the development, in the coast of the Gulf of Mexico, of cultures contemporary to that of Teotihuacán.

This is a similar city to Teotihuacán but smaller and adapted to the tropical environment, that is, it has no network of streets or axes, but buildings scattered according to the irregularities of the terrain. Its pyramids were smaller and built in a less massive style, lighter than those on the plateau.

In this place seven buildings were found for the game of pelota, some decorated with reliefs alluding to the ceremony; besides the reliefs there were monuments depicting pelota players as important people in society who were buried with objects representing their clothing in stone (Photos 74, 75 and 76).

The gods of these people were depicted in pottery. Some, like the rain god, were the same in the whole mesoamerican area (Photo 78), also the god Xipe (Photo 77), whereas the god Xochipilli (Photo 81), and the god of Death (Photos 82 and 83) were regional creations.

Monte Albán

Development in the Oaxacan area was also similar to that of Teotihuacán, the most typical city in that area being Monte Albán; this city was built on a hill which was

(85) Mythological scenes were depicted on Maya plates.

(86) (87) These figurines are from the island of Jaina in Campeche, considered to be a cemetery.

(88) The priest-rulers of the Mayas were buried in luxurious tombs with sarcophagi of stone decorated with ritual scenes.

(89) Maya stele
depicting a
person of the
ruling class
opposite a
smaller
subordinate.

(90) Two Maya
personages,
an important
woman and
a governor make
an offering of
a tiger's head.

(91) (92) These Maya heads accompanied the personage buried in the tomb of Palenque, Chis., the typical features of the Mayas can be appreciated.

(93) The Maya sun god also accompanied the personage buried in Palenque.

(94) The Maya sun god was Visco who had a shark's tooth.

(95) In maya architecture, these decorated tablets were used, on which dates can be read.

(96) The tiger was an animal much worshipped among the Maya groups, they gave him the name of Balam.

(97) The Mayas represented their rulers in large monuments as well as in small pieces of sculpture.

(98) Chaac the Maya god of the rain is depicted on this stone slab.

(99) In the inside of the temples were great tablets with engravings representing gods and priests with hieroglyphics which have not yet been deciphered.

(100) A small male figure from Jaina. Campeche.

adapted to the city planning. The centre of economic, religious, and political control was situated on the highest part and made up of buildings and pyramids for temples dedicated to different gods.

Around the control area were the palaces of the governing body. In some of these, tombs for burial were built under the floors. (Photo 108).

The parts most distant from the centre were inhabited by merchants and craftsmen and outside in the surrounding valleys lived the peasants who maintained the city, which was the same as in Teotihuacán.

The zapotecs had extraordinarily good pottery, besides vessels of diverse beautiful forms (Photo 104) used for exchanging and as offerings which represented their deities as in the "13 serpent" (Photo 103), the god Tlacuache (Photo 107), some deities in the shape of birds (Photo 111) and tigers (Photo 109) were typical of this region, on the other hand the god Xipe (Photo 106) and the rain god were the same as in the mesoamerican regions.

They also did some fine work in hard stone, this mask representing the Bat god being a good example (Photo 110).

The Maya Culture

The maya societies that developed in the low lands were quite different as regards the material expression (pottery) of their social processes from the societies existing on the plateau during this period of time; nevertheless apart from these and other geographical, physical, and linguistic differences, the types of social organization and their changes coincided basically throughout the mesoamerican area.

In the vast territory of the mayas, there were a series of cities:

On the shores of rivers; in the Petén tropical forest; in the mountains of Chiapas and Guatemala, and on the plateau of the Yucatán peninsula.

Some cities like Tikal in Guatemala were great urban centres with a population of up to 45000 inhabitants and stretching over 16 sq. metres. Although these centres were in general smaller, they controlled a series of surrounding villages from which they received tribute.

The maya cities lived in a state of conflict and competition with each other which is obvious from their drawings and sculptures which have been found. This provoked a highly developed ideological structure which functioned mainly as an element of cohesion and social control supported by warrior control.

Perhaps the first artistic expression known in the

(101) Grotesque face in stucco found at Comalcalco, Tabasco.

(102) Ceremonial brazier with the image of the sun god.

mesoamerican territory belongs to these maya groups, both in architectural styles and in sculpture, painting and pottery. Each maya city was distinguished by some exceptional creation, each maya centre had its own special development in some of these arts, for example, the architecture and planning of Tikal has no peer and the stucco decoration at Palenque is unique; the ornamented lintels at Yaxchilán are particularly outstanding (Photo 95) the Puuc style decorated buildings like those in the city of Uxmal; the statuettes of the isle of Jaina, so typical and exclusive; in brief, each maya centre had its speciality in artistic creation although a certain unifying element can be appreciated.

It must not be forgotten that in spite of the differences in material representation in the maya area and in the remaining areas of mesoamerica, the economic, political and ideological patterns were basically the same, what changed was the way of representing them, but not the function of these elements.

For example, the maya pyramids like those on the plateau, were massive bodies, terraced, without any internal spaces, built to support small temples which were closed precincts where the image of the god was kept, and to which only the priest-rulers and their closest assistants had access. The people remained below in the enormous squares that stretched out in front of the pyramids. In the case of the maya temples these were highly adorned and decorated with stucco, paintings and sculptures; on the upper part of the temple a "cresting" was built to give the building extra height.

The administrative buildings were constructed in a different way, there were rooms and corridors covered with a false or jutty roof, typical of all the maya area, it was a sort of triangular archway, this tecnique gave greater possibilities to interior spaces than in the buildings in the plateau regions. In the interior of these temples, especially in the one at Palenque, were great tablets with engravings depicting their gods and priests (Photo 99) on these they wrote texts which still have not been deciphered. Also at Palenque, in the so called Temple of the Inscriptions, a tomb was found inside the pyramid, which was a unique case in mesoamerica, as the pyramids were not generally used as tombs but as places of

(103) 13 serpent was the name of this goddess related to agriculture in the Oaxaca region.

(104) This ceramic box has on it the symbol of water; it was probably used in some temple for ritual purposes.

(105) Clay urn dedicated to the god Xipe.

(106) *The god Xipe was adopted by almost all mesoamerican groups; it was related to vegetation.*

(107) *Tlacuache was a god connected with maize.*

worship (Photo 88). In this case there was a stone sarcophagus covered with a large tablet dated 692 A.D. with engravings related to concepts of life and death.

The body buried there must have been that of an important person in Palenque as he had a mask and many jade and shell jewels, two fine stucco heads were also buried with him having the typical maya features (Photos 91 and 92) and a jade sun god (Photo 93).

Maya designs and motifs depicted in their crafts and buildings were like those of the other mesoamerican people, imposed and manipulated by the ruling class, the artist could not express himself freely as the rulers used objets d'art in order to transmit concepts which would strengthen their position. (Photo 84).

The mayas were splendid craftsmen; they made entire table services in ceramic pottery decorated with mythological scenes in fine colours (Photo 85).

Their Jaina statuettes tell of the marked social stratification that existed in maya society; the priest-rulers dressed luxuriously, decorated their faces with scarifications and wore very complicated hairstyles. (Photos 86 and 87).

They portrayed their rulers (Photo 97) and gods in different materials and in different shapes. (Photos 98 and 96).

(108) *The state rulers were buried in luxurious tombs with paintings on the walls, ceramic offerings, and accompanying gods.*

The highest grades of knowledge in pre-hispanic mesoamerica were attained by the mayas. Through their vegisimal system of mathematics they succeeded in handling the solar calender of 360 days with 5 extra days, and also a ritual calender of 260 days. They knew the behaviour of certain planets such as Venus, and valued the equinoxes and solstices believing that the sun moved round the earth.

They had a record of time called the "Cuenta larga" where they had fixed a special date which coincided with the beginning of their world and they dated all their monuments and writings on their manuscripts counting from this date.

Their mathematical system was vegisimal and the value of a number was given by the position it had; they used the "O" to point out position, although they did not use it to signify the absence of value. They wrote many manuscripts which were destroyed at the time of the conquest, in which they registered historical facts and stories of original myths, and also part of their history. Only a few of these were rescued, the vast majority being lost. Up to the present time no one has been able to read maya writing although their numerals have been well understood.

(109) The Zapotecs depicted gods and sacred animals on urns or ceramic vessels.

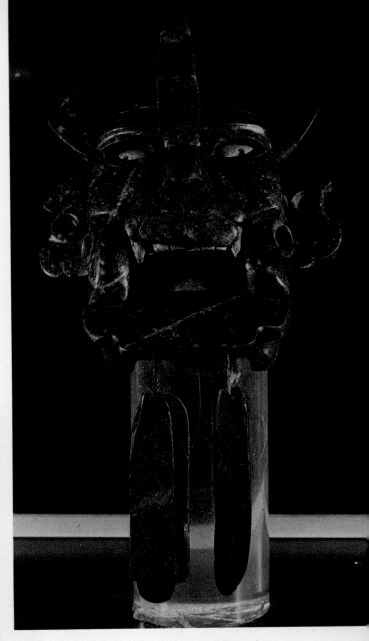

(110) A mask made out of green stone and shell mosaic representing the bat god, typical of the Zapotecs.

The disintegration of the States

The Teotihuacan system and its control centre, the most important in mesoamerica, disintegrated around the year 700 A.D. archaeological research indicating that the causes of this were manifold.

On the one hand, the city of Teotihuacán had grown out of proportion, inside there was no food producing basis from which to feed the urban area, therefore they depended on the exploitation of the peasants in the surroundings. The

greater demand for food and labour for the city from the peasantry provoked a crisis which brought about problems and fomented tension between city and countryside causing an imbalance in the state organization.

On the other hand, however, contemporary to Teotihuacán in the same plateau area, there already existed two cities that rivalled it — Cholula and Xochicalco.

These two cities took advantage of the break up of the situation in Teotihuacán of which they were the partial promotors, bringing pressure to bear in their trade dealings, and intervening in villages dominated by Teotihuacán.

This crisis was not only felt in Teotihuacán but in many regions of mesoamerica.

The climate of tension created in mesoamerica after the disintegration of Teotihuacán was resolved by the formation of military states which economically worked in the same way as those formerly considered to be theocratic in type. The relationship between the exploited and the exploiting class and the great socioeconomic division between the people of the city and those of the country prevailed, but control was exercised basically by the military body, although religious norms were also of great importance. The crisis also provoked the regrouping of the population in smaller centres and in raised areas for protection, with walls or surrounded by ditches as in Xochicalco. In the case of the central plateau the disintegration

(111) This large urn made of clay represents a priest who, on his headdress bears the figure of a god in the shape of a bird.

(112) This Chac-Mool appeared in Ihuatzio. Michoacán.

(113) The presence of the warrior image on sculpture corresponds to the climate of tension provoked by the disintegration of the state of Teotihuacán when the military states became the best solution.

of the city of Teotihuacán dispersed groups who settled in the best places within the area formerly controlled by the state. One of the results of this was the fortifying of Cholula and Xochicalco which controlled first the Puebla-Tlaxcala valleys and secondly the great fertile valley of Morelos.

Tula

The only possibility for other displaced groups was to gather together and settle in the north of the plateau. Thus rose the city of Tula, a centre controlling the northern area. This city had a large population organized on a basis of social stratification; but it was not like Teotihuacán nor did it have an obvious central power. When less than 50% of its inhabitants produced food, experience showed that a city like Teotihuacán could not survive those conditions.

Toltec architecture followed to a large extent the patterns of Teotihuacán, but it was of less quality as regards constructive techniques; the pyramids for the temples were smaller, the palaces less spacious and badly built. However, there were elements in the decoration which gave a special high light to the architecture. The entrance to some temples was formed by porticoes in the shape of a plumed serpent, and to hold up the roof of the temple they used columns depicting warriors. (Photo 113).

They developed some new elements in architecture such as colonnades and pilasters to hold up roofs. The superstructure of the pyramids was decorated with reliefs portraying tigers and eagles eating hearts. The walls surrounding the pyramids had reliefs of scenes to do with Death. Such decorative elements had not been seen in so great a profusion before this period, which would indicate that war themes then became predominant. Although the military structure became predominant, Tula was also an agricultural village depending on the rains for survival, so people went on worshipping the god Tlaloc who at this time was also Lord of the Mountains (Photo 117).

Another deity was Chac-Mool who appeared in Tula for the first time; this god was depicted as a reclining person dressed as a warrior who acted as the divine messenger. The sculpture of statuary was quite developed in Tula with war and death elements constantly appearing.

In their luxury crafts they also made clay figures of warriors and on some occasions they covered them with shell mosaic (Photo 115).

At that time the exchange of craft products with distant groups from Guatemala and El Salvador became more intense, there they made a special sort of ceramic which has been termed "leaded" due to its metalic reflection (Photo 120); this was in great demand in all mesoamerica.

(114) Chac-Mool or messenger is a warrior god who originated at this time.

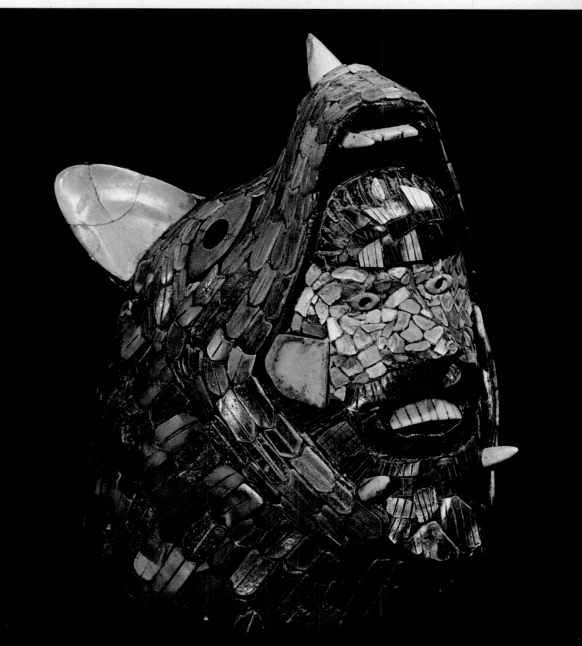

(115) Warrior themes are repeated in Toltec artisanry; this is a ceramic figure covered with shell mosaic.

(116) *Polychromed telamon originally supporting an altar.*

(117) *Worship of the god Tlaloc continued in Tula but with less intensity than in Teotihuacán and with the variation that his shrines are in the mountains where it was thought the rain originally came from.*

(118) *The Huastecs occupied the northern area of the gulf coast, their principal god was Quetzalcoatl who is sometimes depicted as an adolescent.*

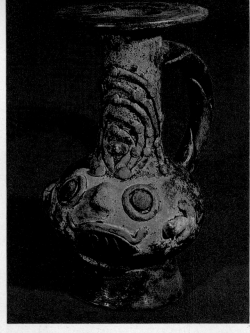

(119) This polished alabaster carving shows the perfection reached by manual technique.

(120) One of the commercial objects found in the whole mesoamerican area was the leaden ceramic produced in El Salvador and Guatemala; this piece was found in Tula.

(121) Occasionally this same god Quetzalcoatl was depicted dead with his heart out and a skull on his headdress.

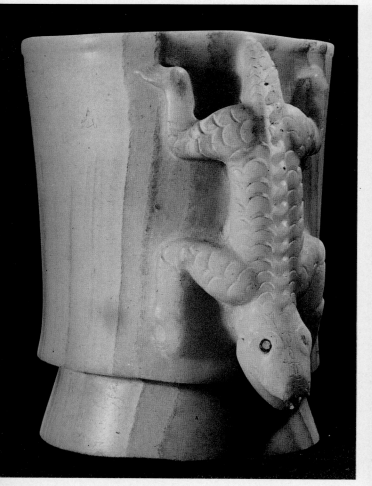

(122) These shell-ornaments were sewn onto the blankets of the rulers; on these appears Quetzalcoatl in different attitudes.

(123) The decoration on this Mixtec vase is the same as that found on the manuscripts.

(124) Ceramic continued to be the most important mode of expression of the mesoamerican groups.

(125) Resin (copal) was used in certain rites; this was burned in these censers.

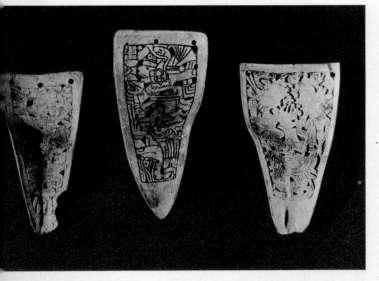

(126) Polychromed anthropomorphic vase in Mixtec-Puebla style.

(127) Tomb 7 at Monte Albán, Oax. is one of the few that have been found intact. A ruler was buried here covered in gold and turquoise jewels, with ceramic objects and rock crystal.

(128) The carving and polishing of alabaster implied a technical knowledge and a manual ability resulting from a long tradition of craftsmanship.

The Huastecs

In the coastal region of the gulf when Tajín lost its domination of the area, there arose the group known as Huastecs who controlled an extensive part of that region.
Its centres were small and walled. There were administrative buildings and pyramids for its different deities, many of them circular and dedicated to the god Quetzalcóatl (Photo 118), its main patron.
For their sculptures the huastecs used stone from the region which was white limestone and on this stone they depicted different views of the god Quetzalcóatl and other gods. (Photo 121).

The ruling class used gold and shell ornaments and dressed differently from the common people who in that region went nude. (Photo 122).

In the huastec area pottery figures of humans and animals were made (Photo 124) which were also used as offerings at the tombs of important people.

The Mixtecs

In the Oaxaca area during the stage of the military states, the mixtec group evolved. The mixtec population centres were small, but they had similar characteristics to those throughout mesoamerica.

They controlled the central valleys of Oaxaca, the same ones that had been dominated by Monte Albán. They utilized the ruins of the ancient city and buried mixtec personages in their tombs. Among these zapotec tombs with mixtec people in them mention must be made of tomb number seven (of Monte Albán) which was found to be exceptionally intact. It was possible to recover all their treasure which is now on show at the Oaxaca museum. The Anthropological museum has a reproduction of this tomb on show in Mexico (Photo 127).

The mixtec crafts are among the finest in mesoamerica, luxury ceramic pottery was decorated with the finest designs, like those found in the holy books or manuscripts (Photos 123 and 125). More than 20 of these manuscripts are in existence at the present time, illustrating with lovely drawings, sometimes history and sometimes the mixtec mythology. Alabaster vases used for trading with other groups were of great value as they were technically very difficult to make (Photo 128), also there were objects made of rock crystal (Photo 130).

Metal work was only used for making decoration and never for tools, food production or arms. The models and techniques were not original to mesoamerica, but produced by contacts with central American groups where there definitely existed a tradition of metal work. (Photo 131).

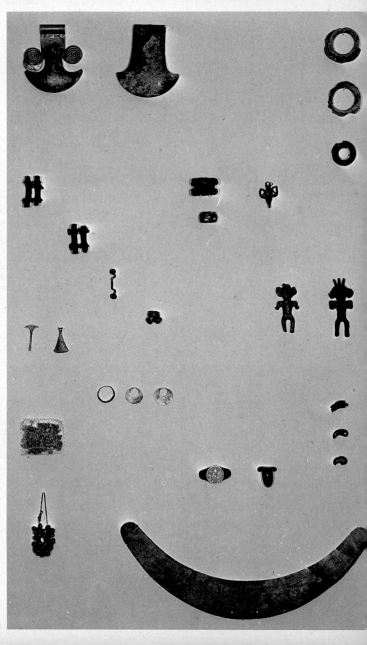

(129) The prehispanic peoples of Mesoamerica used two types of drums: vertical and horizontal, like these which the Aztecs called huehuetl.

(130) Pieces of rock crystal were much appreciated due to their scarcity and the technical difficulties involved in shaping it.

(131) In Mesoamerica metals were not used for making work tools, they were only used for objects of decoration.

(132) The habit of smoking tobacco originated in prehispanic Mesoamerica.

(133) The largest quantity of metal objects was found in the western region; this copper mask represents the god Xipe.

(134) These small vessels were given as offerings at the burial of children.

(135) (136) The Tarasco rulers used gold, shell and obsidian pectorals, earrings and ornaments.

(137) This sculpture known as The Queen of Uxmal formed part of a building.

(138) A corpulent personage wearing a cotton breast plate.

Western Mexico

The foundation of military states generally followed the disintegration of the theocratic states, but in the case of the western region of mesoamerica no transformation of incipient agricultural societies into theocratic states was observed, instead, they continued at this stage of development for much longer.

In about the XII century, the integration of a group of villages into larger units was observed in the area, along with the appearance of control centres which did not exist formerly. In general these elements of transformation noted here corresponded to the first stage of the early states, except that in this case they were already military in type. The most important control centre in this region was called Tzintzuntzan, in what is now the state of Michoacán. The religious buildings were circular with a rectangular addition; these were known as "yácatas". This centre was situated on the shores of lake Patzcuaro where Chinampas were constructed. It is outstanding that these groups in the west of Mexico, the Tarascos, had considerable contact with South American peoples as shown in the craft metal work (Photos 133, 135 and 136) and pottery (Photo 134).

The Maya Area

The maya area, as an integral part of the mesoamerican area, also suffered a series of transformations throughout the 9th century A.D. as a result of the disintegration of the control centres which the former state had held.

The situation in the maya area was similar to that in the Central Plateau, in that the people were grouped in smaller walled centres, and there was a fundamentally warrior control, as always upheld by ideological elements. Centres such as Tikal, Copán, Quirigua, Palenque and others were almost abandoned and in ruins due to the effects of the jungle environment, as the people who remained living there did not use and maintain the buildings as before as they did not hold the same meaning and furthermore they were unable to do so, whereas in some of the northern cities in the peninsula of Yucatán such as Chichén Itzá, Uxmal and others received more people and enlarged the old centres with buildings in another style and in general under other concepts; they stopped using the "Cuenta Larga" system, and no more cresting and stucco was used architecturally.

The instance of the city of Chichén Itzá is a special one; the old part of the city is in classical maya style however the new constructions belonging to this period are in a very similar style to that of Tula in the Central Plateau having porticoes in the shape of plumed serpents, telamons, Chac-Mools, colonnades and similar decorative

(139) (140) These objects were found in an underground natural reservoir of water at Chichen-Itzá where women were sacrificed in honour of the god of water.

elements, processions of jaguars and eagles eating human hearts, warriors in the toltec manner, censers for Tlaloc, etc., but such maya features as the false roof still persisted.

During this period the mayas carried on doing excellent sculpture, painting, and metal work (Photos 139 and 140), pottery (Photos 141 and 142), and also wrote magnificent sacred books.

Chichén lost power over its control area and Mayapán became the most important control centre in the northern area of the peninsula around the year 1290. This was a city of some 9 sq. kms. with a population of 12 000 inhabitants and completely walled. There was a small Temple to Kukulkan which was the plumed serpent; this cult had supposedly been brought by the toltecs. There was no pelota game here and the centre did not have a very prominent role.

After Mayapán there were no more important control centres in the maya area, as there were no unifying elements which had existed in the Plateau when the Aztec state was formed. When the Spaniards arrived in this area they found a series of small domains in a state of disunion and in constant struggle one with another.

The Central Plateau

In the XIII century, the Central Plateau was divided into a series of small states — more than 60 of them — scattered throughout a vast territory and on the shores of the Great

(141) This vessel is typical of the Mayas of the last prehispanic period.

(142) This figure representing a priest is from Mayapán, the walled city.

(143) The Aztecs developed a military state based economically on tribute. War was one of their most important institutions as through this they extended the territory under their domination.

Mexican Lake. These groups lived in conflict one with another, always waging war to possess more land and to gain commercial control over certain areas.

The centres situated on the shores of the lake had many advantages: water transport and fertile areas on the shore, fish and vegetables near at hand; thus it was for these reasons that there were frequent struggles for control of these areas.

The hegemony of the states changed, sometimes falling to Culhuacán, after to Azcapotzalco, and finally to Mexico-Tenochtitlan which became the most important city on the whole Plateau initially through its alliances with Texcoco and Tlacopan.

The states unified to form a much stronger one and thus were able to conquer and control the rest. After a short time, Mexico-Tenochtitlan stood alone as the strongest state and absorbed all the production of the colonies it had conquered without sharing with Texcoco and Tlacopan.

When the mexicas became the most important people in the Plateau area, they wrote a history of their origins on manuscripts; it was the history of a pilgrimage in search of a place to settle, and the vicissitudes suffered during the pilgrimage were all related. They were said to have come from a mythical place called "Aztlán", from which the name Aztecs comes; they wandered for many years until they reached the Mexico valley and settled in Chapultepec where they lived for some years (Photo 145).

They left Chapultepec and finally came upon an island in the middle of the Mexico lake where, on an indian fig tree an eagle was devouring a serpent; this was the sign given to them by their god Huitzilopochtli for the founding of their city.

This was the official version of the history and origin of the mexicas and very difficult to verify archaeologically.

According to historical sources their first king was Acamapichtli and after there were eight more who devoted themselves to conquering other lands and subjecting many peoples from whom they had demanded tribute.

In a short time, the mexicas or aztecs, through these conquests had increased their economic, political and military power. They extended their dominion to Oaxaca, the Gulf coastline and the entire region of the Central Plateau. When a village was conquered, they left behind a group of representatives of the mexican state to collect the tribute consisting of local food products, raw materials or craft work.

The representatives sent the produce to the control centres which the government had throughout the territory, and these in their turn sent it to Mexico-Tenochtitlan. The warriors who upheld the framework of the state saw to it that all orders were carried out (Photo 143).

The development of the city was well planned and the surface area of the island enlarged using the chinampas system, that is reclaiming land from the lake by means of

(144) This monument known as "the stone of Tizoc" commemorated the conquests of this Mexican governor.

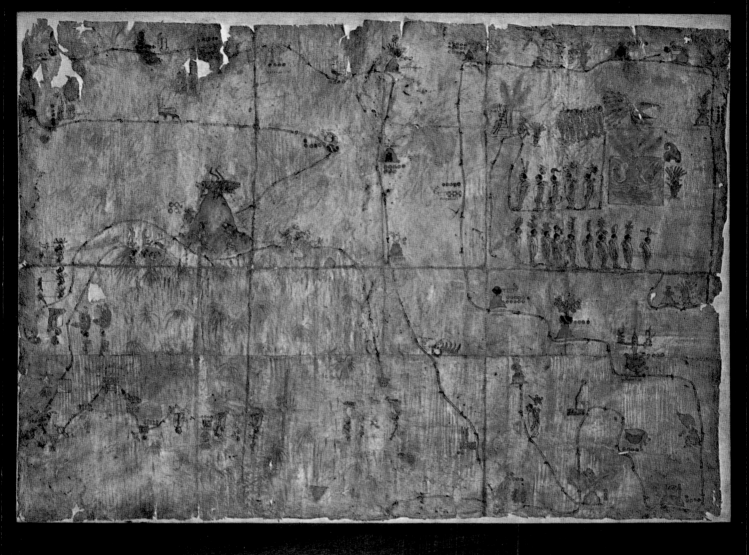

(145) The Mexicas recorded their own history in several documents relating their origins and the foundation of Tenochtitlan up to the time of the conquest.

(146) To commemorate the warlike and conquering deeds of the Aztec or Mexica rulers, great monuments were sculpted in their honour.

65

(147) The sun god, Huizilopochtli was the first among the Mexicas,
and to survive needed human sacrifice. The Mexicas
then organized wars to get prisoners and tear their hearts out.

(148) The hearts of the scrificial victims were placed in this sacred
vase as an offering to the sun.

artificial islets on canals through which they travelled by
canoe.

The centre of the city was occupied by the great teocali or
ceremonial area where the religious buildings stood. The
most important of these was a double pyramid in which
one chamber was dedicated to Tlaloc, the ancient Rain
god, and the other to the god Huitzilopochtli, the god of
the Sun and war. There were more temples dedicated to
the remaining gods in the Mexican pantheon. In this area
there were pelota games and the Tzompantli which was a
depositary for the skulls of those who had died by human
sacrifice, and also the Calmecac or boarding school for the
young noblemen.

All this area dedicated to religion was surrounded by a
wall covered with snakes having three entrances connec-
ting the area with the great roadways which went across
the lake to the main land. Outside the great teocali were
the state administrative buildings and the area of the palaces inhabited by the ruling class (the piltin); outside this
area lived the common people, (the macehualtin) on the
chinampas.

observed the situation and the vulnerability of the villages, and so the warriors were better able to plan their attacks against other groups. Besides their warlike activities which were very intense, the mexicas created an important group of architects specialized in jewellery, ceramics, gems, and the art of feathers, also workmen for public works whom they controlled and obliged to work for the state so as to reinforce ideology and keep the ruling class in power.

The imposing architecture of the city, the planning itself, the hydraulic undertakings necessary to contain to waters of the lake, the great quantity of sculptures they possessed, the crafts, religious ideas and knowledge were all elements which helped to strengthen the system.

Originally the city was divided into four large sections or districts and these were divided into calpullis or suburbs which were basic self-sufficient units managed by the state.

The calpulli were situated in land of common ownership each family in the unit was linked by blood ties and worked on a section of the land in the calpulli, from there they got their food and had to pay tribute, they also had to work on other land whose produce was exclusively for the benefit of the rulers.

Every calpulli had its school, a house where the tribute was administered, a place where justice was dealt with, a temple, and a palace where the noble lived. In the XVI century there were more than 20 calpullis functioning.

In Tlatelolco, a town near to Tenochtitlan there was a large market where produce from all regions of mesoamerica was exchanged (Photo 151); this was dealt with by the traders who occupied a very important place in society, as, besides trading, they served the state by acting as spies; during their business transactions they

(151) The market at Tlatelolco was the largest and most important in the centre of Mexico; there, objects from all parts of Mesoamerica were exchanged and courts of justice were held.

(152) Copper bell used as an ornament.

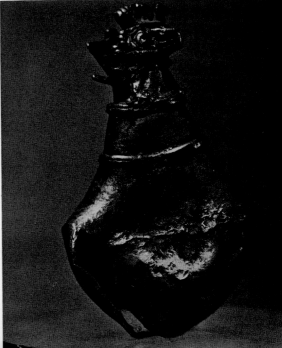

Each mexican ruler commemorated his deeds in magnificently worked monuments (Photo 146) which were placed in the most prominent places in the control centres. The state controlled ideology, mainly from the religion which was of a complex nature. There were creator gods (Photo 155), sun gods and war gods such as Huitzilopochtli who needed human sacrifice in order to continue shedding light on the earth (Photo 147). Prisoners captured in the wars were sacrificed and their heart torn out; this was put into a great stone vessel (Photo 148); in this way the rulers justified their policy of conquest.

There were wind gods (Photo 154), gods of agriculture (Photos 158 and 159), the god of flowers and song (Photo 160) and images of sacred animals such as the

(153) The Mexican century was of
52 years at the end of which
they believed that the sun would
not come out again. When a new
century began they sculpted
a monument symbolizing
the century that had ended.

(154) Ehecatl was the name of the god
of the wind, occasionally he was
depicted in the shape of
a monkey, but he always had
a bird's beak for a mouth.

(155) The mother god of the Aztecs
was Coatlicue, she had given birth
to Huitzilopochtli who was also
the sun, to Coyolxauhqui who was
the moon and to all the stars.

69

(156) Sculpture of a Mexican man.

(157) The mother god, Coatlicue, was portrayed in many different ways. This figure was found in Puebla.

snake (Photo 163). The cult to these lesser deities was more accessible to the vast majority of mexicas.

They also made fantastic animals such as the Ahuizotl or water dog, a wicked being that lived in the lakes, whose tail ended in a hand, and with this he grabbed at children who came near (Photo 162).

Sometimes the sculptures had toponymical meanings as

(158) All the prehispanic sculptures were painted in different colours although very few have preserved them. This is the god Napatecuhtli, one of the gods of agriculture.

(159) Although warrior gods predominated in this society, the deities of agriculture and maize were also important.

in the case of Chapulin (Photo 164) (Chapultepec). Some members of the ruling class were devoted to science, mathematics, astronomy and medicine.

They used the mesoamerican calendar which had worked for centuries, that is, two calendars, one solar with 360 days plus 5 complementary days and another calendar of 260 days. The solar one had 8 months of 20 days and each day and month was dedicated to an important god. When the two calendar rotations which had begun on a certain date began to coincide in their initial dates, then a century had passed, that is 52 solar years (Photo 153).

In the course of this cycle, they held a ceremony called "The new fire" in which a fire was lit and thanks given to the sun for having granted the mexicans another century of life.

Suddenly the development process in mesoamerica was interrupted, and the European conquest caused a complete change in the old structures.

160) *Xochipilli means the lord of the flowers; he was considered the god of song and of flowers.*

161) *The coyote was made divine and his hide changed into beautiful feathers.*

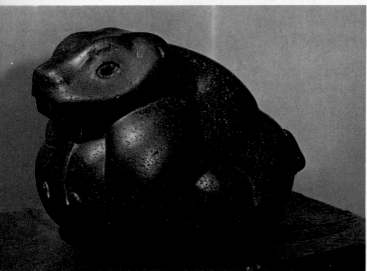

(162) The name of this animal was Ahuizotl or water dog; this was a mythological being who inhabited the lakes.

(163) In prehispanic mythology the serpent was related to the forces of nature; this is the image of a rattle snake.

(164) This carved precious stone is a three dimensional representation of Chapultepec or, Cerro del Chapulín.

UNIT II.
THE EUROPEAN CONQUEST

The Spanish conquest of Mexico represented a confrontation of two types of social organization at different stages of development; on the one hand, a group of villages, a great number of which were subjected to the Aztec state and the remainder grouped together in different ways and with different social levels; on the other, the Spanish state, a European power, with a feudal organization, a superior technology, and a series of economic necessities which impelled it to embark upon this venture.

The situation in Spain in the XVI century

Spain, in the XVI century was at a political and economic disadvantage in comparison with the other powers with which it was engaged in keen commercial competition; the other powers were more developed, thus Spain had to buy goods from them and became gradually poorer.

Out of this trade war was born the search for new trade routes on the part of Spain, and an expedition to the Indies was planned. The result of this situation was the discovery of America and after, the conquest and colonization of some of its regions.

THE SITUATION IN MEXICO

For the prehispanic societies, the conquest meant a confrontation of two totally different concepts of the world and two different technologies; the Spanish one logically having all the advantages. (Photos 165 and 166).

After the excesses perpetrated during the first period of the conquest during which the Europeans devoted themselves to sacking the mineral wealth and destroying prehispanic models wholesale, the conquerors tried to replace these by European elements and here, religion played a key role.

The Colony

The Spanish crown began exploiting the population and the local resources in a more organized way than the prehispanic rulers, especially in the extraction of metals; they also began extensive exploitation of arable land.

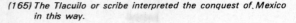
(165) The Tlacuilo or scribe interpreted the conquest of Mexico in this way.

(166) The shape and manufacturing technique of this vase are totally prehispanic; however, the decoration is European in style.

They also began to build cities, with of course, native man power from those who had been dispossessed of their lands, and who were now workers and servants.

During the period of colonization, Spain based its wealth on New Spain, but what it really did was to make the country even more behind in general industrialization than the rest of Europe. This process brought about the fact that the riches extracted from the Indies fell almost directly into the hands of England, Holland, France, and Italy which were industrial powers from which, as has been stated, Spain bought all the goods she consumed and even those needed by her colonies. These demands caused New Spain to be exploited to an even higher degree.

Contact with Spain brought about a series of changes in the native villages, depending on the circumstances in which the groups found themselves, for example, proximity to control centres, geographical differences or those superficially to do with the extraction of products the Spaniards had decided upon, these situations brought about different levels of integration into the Spanish mode and therefore produced a great variety of ways of life for the indians.

Some of these communities were almost completely absorbed by the Spanish groups and lost their prehispanic culture patterns.

Others, more distant from the dominant groups, were subjected to a different process; these underwent exploitation mainly through religion during the early stages of the colony and then were left to develop hybrid patterns almost without any alien intervention, due to distance and inaccessability. They also preserved, thanks to this distance, some prehispanic patterns such as the language, ways of feeding. craft models, some rites, deities, but there are few phenomena certain to be of prehispanic origin. Moreover, almost all the natives were converted to Christianity which changed their behaviour, customs, and daily life, and gave them a new and different morality which became reflected in all their material expressions.

The present day situation

The result of the interrelation of all these elements produced during the conquest is that at the present time there exists in Mexico an extremely wide range of native com-

(167) At the present time the indigenous groups are confined to the most remote and barren areas of the country.

munities, different from each other and with diametrically opposed concepts of life. From Independence to the present day, there have been many political changes in Mexico, and in spite of the considerable amount of effort put into integration, protection and understanding of the native problem of late, the Mexican indians continue to be the most exploited group in the country.

In the following chapter of this study, on ethnology, there is a list of the most representative indigenous groups in Mexico showing their customs.

It is interesting to point out that some contemporary communities are the living example of the domination and exploitation of one group by another just as in the XVI century.

UNIT III. ETHNOGRAPHY
The distribution of indigenous groups in Mexico. (Photo 167)

In the mesoamerican area, there is now a native population fluctuating between 6 and 8 million people. In the state of Chiapas are the groups known as mayenses, tzeltales, tzotziles, lacandones, choles and tojolabales; in Oaxaca the most important native groups are the mixtecs, zapotecs, huaves, chinantecs, mazatecs, mixes and triques; in Guerrero live the amusgos, nahuas

and chapines; in Michoacan are the tarascos or purepechas. In the states of Nayarit and Jalisco live the huichol and cora people and on a lesser scale, the people of the tepehuanes who came from Durango; in Sonora live the seri, mayo, yaqui and papajo peoples, and in Chihuahua the tarahumaras and quicapus.

(The foregoing classification is linguistic, as this characteristic has been the least spoilt in all the native population).

In the gulf area there is a predominantly totonac population; in San Luis de Potosí the main groups are the huastecs, potosinos, and nahuas; to the south of Veracruz live the popoluca and nahuatl people; the chontales live in Tabasco and although they bear the same name, do not form part of the chontal group who live in Chiapas; in the lowlands of the Yucatán peninsula live groups of mayas. In the central part of mesoamerica there are other important enclaves such as the Puebla mountains with their nahuatl, totonaca and otomi peoples. In the states of Querétaro, México and Hidalgo live the otomis, mazahuas and matzaltlincas; and finally to the north of San Luis Potosí there is a small population of pames.

The Economy

Agriculture is the basic economic activity among the natives. Native economy is subsistence in type, that is, only enough is produced for home consumption and rarely is there any surplus; if there is, the product is taken to market through intermediaries and after terrible exploitation by the half-castes, ladinos or even the natives. An example of this was found among the mixes and zapotecs. The main products are maize, beans, marrows and chiles. In this sector prehispanic techniques are still conserved (cultivation using the coa); some native groups adopted the plough but their economic means did not allow them, on many occasions to have a pair of animals to draw it. Agricultural technique really largely depends on each place and its environment. (Photos 168 and 172).

In the wooded areas, for example, among the totonacs of Veracruz, the lacandones at Chiapas, the mayas at Quintana Roo, more or less the same procedure is followed, trees are cut down after they are cleaned and the brush is burned, the resulting ash serves as fertilizer for the earth; once the burning is finished they begin to work on the land and dig furrows. Each family stores the grain it is going to need for the whole year, the best being selected for sowing the following year. It is important to mention the fact that the whole family takes part in the sowing, so when teachers complain about the poor school atten-

dance or when the ladino, Spanish or national citizens call the natives apathetic for not wanting to have any education, they fail to take into account that the school calendars coincide with the agricultural ones and if the children don't help in the agricultural work of their parents, the native economy would break down.

Women and children follow the father who makes the holes in the ground, they plant the seed and afterwards using their feet they cover it with earth to protect it against the birds and animals of the field.

(168) *Agriculture is the basic economic activity for the natives and is carried out in general with prehispanic techniques, although in some regions where there are cattle the plough is used.*

(169) *The same peasants who cultivated the sugar cane made these grinding machines to make the clayed brown sugar or unrefined sugar used in typical Mexican food.*

(170) *A barn in the Morelos region, known as Cuexcomatl.*

The children also help to scare away pests and to bend the ears of maize so that the crop will not be lost because of the heavy rain. They also tread the earth round each plant to avoid the soil being taken away by the quickly passing water. Once the maize is sown they then proceed to cultivate the tomatoe, beans, peas, and other vegetables in the same maize-field.

Months later comes the gathering, shredding and shelling. These tasks occupy the whole family.

On hillside areas terracing is still used and all available land is cultivated intensively.

In the lakeland areas cultivation of chinampas is used and maximum production is got from very small plots. This now can only be seen in a very few places, one is in the mexican area of lake Mixquic.

The storage of grain

In some native centres the harvest is stored in barns which are independent of the dwelling houses. These have different names depending on the region and the particular type of grain. A type of construction called a troje is used and in the Morelos region they use the cuexcomal (Photo 170), this is built quite high off the ground to keep the damp from the grain. The entrance is almost always from above so that the animals do not eat the grain.

When the harvest is kept in the main body of the house a second floor, a sort of attic, is improvized as it must always be kept above ground.

Sugar cane

The cultivation of sugar cane was introduced during the first colonial period. The largest plantations were in the hot areas, mainly in the states of Veracruz, Chiapas and Morelos where it is still cultivated at the present time. During the aforementioned period the Spaniards refined the sugar using very primitive methods. Clayed brown sugar was obtained which the natives still extract by means of primitive grinding machines built by themselves (Photo 169) with which they squash the cane.

The brown sugar or sugar loaf are unrefined pieces of molasses which are left to set and are used for sweetening traditional drinks such as atole, and food such as tamales.

Fishing

A large section of the mesoamerican native population practises fishing as there are many suitable places for this on the sea coast, on rivers and in the lakeland areas.

Lake fishing

Lake fishing was mainly done by the purepechas of Michoacán and the mexicans of the central area.
Nowadays it is reduced to intensive white fishing at Patzcuaro in Michoacań.

The Tarascos

The tarascos or purepechas use an enormous boat made out of a tree trunk. This is possible thanks to their privileged geographical position. They have lands and woods which allow them to build these boats (Photo 173) to hunt and to cultivate, compared with the otomi groups from the Mezquital valley where there is no water and agriculture is impossible.

(171) The natives living in lakeland areas use the chinchorro or large net for smaller fish, but when fishing for sharks they use harpoons and metal hooks.

(172) This hand made plough with a metal tip is used with a mule or oxen.

(173) In the lakeland
      region of Michoacan
      they make canoes
      out of a single
      tree trunk for fishing.
      The most important
      product is white fish.

(174) The Lacandones
      from the Chiapas
      forest still use
      the bow and arrows
      for hunting, and
      the Naza or rigid net
      for river fishing.

(175) *The making of ceramic in the native villages at the present time is in the hands of the womenfolk.*

On the banks of lake Patzcuaro and on the island of Janitzio, the tarascos obtain white fish which is in great demand for the home market and abroad. The White fish at Patzcuaro is the most important economic activity and the village's greatest source of income.

The catch has slowly decreased due to the massive invasion of weed which is destroying all the fauna in the lake, and to contamination which besides Patzcuaro is affecting all lakes rivers and seas, and consequently the native groups who depend on these sources. Other groups, the tepehuatl, chinanteco and mazateco also fish extensively in the rivers.

Although they were more closely related historically to groups from the south west of the United States, the seris share certain cultural features with the mesoamerican groups. In the prehispanic period they lived of the Isla Tiburón and on the coasts of Sonora. They fished for sharks, turtle, and prawns and used a small net known as a ladle net, and a harpoon probably made of reed. Nowadays they use the small drag net or casting net, a large net of colonial origin, also the primitive harpoon made by themselves but now with a metal head or hook. Harpoon fishing is an important characteristic activity of the seris and can be said to be their main source of livelihood.

Harpoon fishing

Fishing is very important in the aridamerican area. As it is impossible to cultivate the desert and sandy areas, groups such as the seris were obliged to subsist by hunting, fishing and cultivation. (Photo 171).

Fishing on the high sea

On the coast of Oaxaca, at Santa María del Mar and San Mateo del Mar, the huaves practise high sea fishing as an alternative to their scant agricultural activity. The fishing catch is sold to the zapotecs in the inland markets.

Ceramics

Ceramic and pottery form an important tradition in Mexico as they have been manufactured locally since the prehispanic period and are still deep-rooted in the population.

(176) In Santa María Atzompa, Oax., the ceramic is fired in sun dried brick ovens.

(177) One of the main crafts in the Yucatán is fibre work, made with ixtle or zapupe fibres which are taken from the trees; with this nose bags, ropes and other things are woven.

(178) The Mixtec indians weave hats, mats, and palm-leaf baskets inside damp caves, in this way the material is kept flexible.

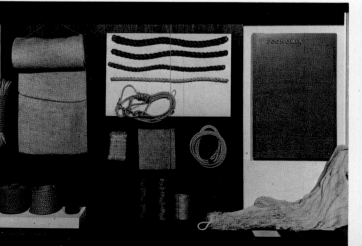

(179) One obvious survival from prehispanic times is to be found in this waist loom from the Otomi region.

Long before the XVI century, there existed a division of labour according to sex, and from this, a division of economic activities which is still in operation, this is that the woman makes the ceramics although she is participating more and more in activities which before were predominantly masculine such as agriculture.

In spite of the enormous production of industrial pottery traditional ceramic is still used, with the exception of certain urban centres.

Throughout almost all the country the woman is responsible for making pottery; the man goes to fetch the clay, kaolin, to far-off areas, and brings it to the woman who prepares and decorates it. Once the woman has made the pot, the men sometimes help to fire it, especially when they are large pieces such as pots or baths called chingonas made by the michoacan women. The men help to load them and fire them in the most primitive way by covering them with logs which gives an irregular firing.

This technique for firing clay used in Michoacán has been substituted in other parts by an oven which gives a more regular finish with no black or burnt parts as in the other method.

In some places the wheel is used which was introduced by the Spaniards. During their period of domination the Spaniards established important pottery centres from which they supplied the colonial élite with products such as the porcelain at Puebla and the ceramic of Dolores Hidalgo and Sayula.

Recently, in some areas, the wheel has been adopted for making pottery and the oven for firing. The oven is used in Oaxaca (Photos 175 and 176) and the man fires the pot that his wife prepares.

Production in many cases is in excess of domestic needs and is therefore suitable for trading. The products are taken to the markets or are exchanged with native groups of the same region like the huastecs who buy objects made by the women of the nahuatl enclave of Chilico, Municipality of Huejutla Hidalgo in the Huastec area. In exchange the nahuatl acquire the huastec nose bags and basket work.

(180) When the weaving of wool was introduced by the Spaniards into Mexico the use of the spinning wheel became necessary.

Rope and basket making

An important complementary activity in these communities is the making of palm leaf accoutrements and agave fibres.

The agave is called Ixtle in the area of Otomí, Zapupe in the Huastec and henequén in the maya area of Yucatán. Nose bags and ropes are made out of agave fibres (Photo 177).

During the colonial period the making of these accoutrements was an important activity. Enormous ropes were used for boats trading with China and Europe. They were also used for packing large quantities of export goods.

Since the prehispanic period this activity has been of importance as these products were used for storing and transporting goods, both on the backs of the macehuales and on mule back by the muleteers.

At the present time there is little production as this fibre is no longer so useful, there are no macehuales who dress in agave fibres and boats and cargo now use ropes made with synthetic materials, the only thing that has survived from the colonial period is the local use of rope

The cultivation of the agave survives for a very small demand. The production centres are mainly the huastec zone, the maya area and the mezquital area. The making of accoutrements is possibly otomí in origin.

The palm industry constitutes a possibility of survival for the natives of the grindingly por mixtec area where erosion has made the earth unproductive after many years of being worked. In Amatlán, Oaxaca, the mixtecs work with palm leaves (Photo 178) in caves to keep them damp, as if they get dry they are impossible to work with and hurt the hands making them bleed.

From the palm leaves baskets, sleeping mats and hats are made. The sleeping mat is used throughout the rural environment, and not only by the natives, instead of a bed. The hat is not a prehispanic element but definitely a national one being a distinctive Mexican article of clothing adopted during colonial times.

Textiles

The production of small clothes is generally in the hands

(181) The native groups in the Oaxaca area used different types of dress and adornment.

of the women who work the mesoamerican waist loom. This type of loom is still used, mainly among the tarascos, mayas and totonacs; the otomi women of Mezquital also use it (Photo 179).

In the area of Mitla, Oaxaca, the greatly increased demand has made them adopt the european pedal loom introduced by the Spaniards together with their agricultural technique, on which coats, blankets and large garments are woven.

Cotton was grown during the prehispanic period and the women twisted the thread with the spindle in the jill and with the waist loom made sashes, shawls, and cloth for making "enredos" (skirts) and quechquémetl (triangular garment).

With the Spaniards settling in the cold lands and the introduction of sheep, woollen garments began to be manufactured as they were costly to import and took a long time to come from Europe. The development of the local textile industry was reflected in a change in the colours of the habits of the Franciscans and the rest of the religious orders; basic changes in clothing came about because of the introduction of local patterns through regional production.

When wool was introduced, a new specific technology was implemented; the spinning wheel appeared (Photo 180) which was used to spin the wool and the pedal loom substituting the waist loom on which it was impossible to

weave all the garments in demand from the Spanish population.

At the present time the tradition of weaving regional garments form cotton with the prehispanic loom is still carried on; sometimes the women buy the thread but mix it double so as to be able to use the waist loom, as the industrial thread is very thin, and so in the very traditional places the women prefer to twist their own thread and then weave it.

The tarahumara loom is a prehispanic survival; this loom is worked standing and not horizontally as is the waist loom. It is the same type of loom as has been found in the south east of the United States, in Indonesia and in India.

Apparel

Apparel is one of the main features which distinguish the mesoamerican groups. The combination of clothes and their colours were generally sufficient to be able to situate the members of a community.

The most characteristic traditional women's dresses are the quechquémetl and the huipil. The quechquémetl the overcoat and the sash are typical of the nahuatl, the totonacs and otomis from the Sierra de Puebla (Photo 183). The sashes are an important element in the apparel of different areas of Oaxaca (Photo 181). The traditional cos-

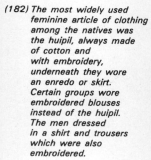

(182) The most widely used feminine article of clothing among the natives was the huipil, always made of cotton and with embroidery, underneath they wore an enredo or skirt. Certain groups wore embroidered blouses instead of the huipil. The men dressed in a shirt and trousers which were also embroidered.

(183) The Nahua, Otomi and Totonac women who lived in the Puebla mountains wore blouses and a quechquemetl which is a triangular garment.

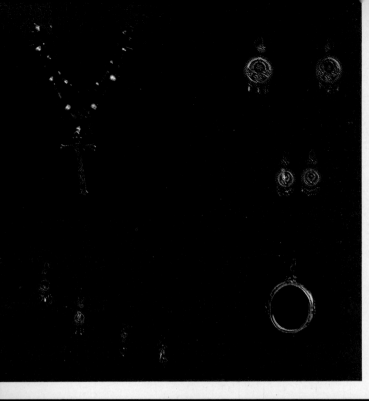

(184) *The jewellery used by the indian women is an element of social and group differentiation.*

(185) *The house is the most important place in the life of the native family, there they are born, celebrate their ceremonies, and watch over their dead.*

(186) *The distribution of the native house varies according to the region. Among the Tarascos, the kitchen is outside and inside are the sleeping mats, an altar and the stóred grain.*

tume of the Chapina woman, from Oaxaca too, is the huipil, which is made from three pieces of cloth joined together cutting out the neck and leaving holes for the arms when sewing it up. (Photo 182).

Jewellery

Jewellery is an accessory to clothes. In the woman they represent social status and her role within the community, probably from prehispanic times.

In Michoacán, the engaged or married woman must wear a necklace which she may not wear as an unmarried woman. (Photo 184).

Included in the native tradition of jewellery, european ele-

(187) In some houses indigenous and hispanic elements are found mixed together as in this type of oven and prehispanic objects such as metate and the three-footed mortar.

(188) The Seri indians of Sonora use pelican skin to cover their cradles like the indians of the south east of the United States.

(189) In the religious festivities the people who have some public office in the community dress in accordance with their function.

(190) Among the Huicholes of Nayarit only the sorcerer, who is the person of greatest prestige in the group, can sit on a chair with a back and use the baton of command.

ments can be found such as colonial beads and silver ornaments.

In Oaxaca, silver jewellery is worn in the shape of medallions used for having engraved upon them images, relics or the catholic cross with symbols of the passion. These religious elements have survived mainly as a european feature adopted by the native woman.

In Mitla at Oaxaca are earrings of the Andalusian type with a marked Moorish influence, also still used among the native women of south east Mexico and Oaxaca are Venetian beads which the Spaniards used for exchange purposes.

The home

The house cum dwelling place plays a very special part in the life of the native communities. It is the most important place: here, the wife gives birth, people gossip, and married couples live together, also it is where the dead are mourned.

In villages and cities home life extends to the market, the church, the mausoleum or the "pulquerías" (the shops where "pulque" drink is sold), but in distant communities where there are none of these places, it is in the home where the old man must sit and transmit the oral tradition, where the old grandmother sits and weaves telling stories.

A section of a maya house shows the domestic tools mainly the most necessary ones. The house is built using

(191) The Lacandones from the Chiapanec forest are perhaps
the most isolated, for this reason they are the ones who have
best preserved their customs.

the materials offered by the environment; in the Sierra de
Puebla and in the Sierra Tarasca the shingle batten or
tejamanil is used; in the maya area, on the coast, in the
low lands, houses are built of straw with roofs of palm
leaves.

The environment does not only determine the materials
but partly the shape of the houses; the maya house is
round, while those of the tarascos are square. Also depending on the climate, some houses have the kitchen and
oven inside and other have it outside. The distribution of
the house goes also according to social organization; the
family nucleus has a different type of dwelling place from
that of an extended family.

The father of the family has a piece of land and when his
children marry he divides up the land and each child
makes his own house on it, but this takes a year and the
daughter in law has to live in the house of her parents in
law or in the nucleus house which is later converted into
an extended house, each woman having her oven. The
house has elements of social organization, and among the
nahuas, totonacs and many communities the construction
of the house is carried out with help from others. Family
friends give one day of work and together they help the

couple to build their house evidencing social cohesion in
this respect. (Photos 185, 186 and 187).

The family

Children in general are always welcome. Although
abortion is practised there is no rejection of children and
in the social organization it is foreseen that a man can
take another wife if he has no children. Among the seris, if
a woman is a widow and has older children, a single man
who could marry a young virgin, prefers to marry the
widow as he sees in the children a potential work
strength.

During the gestation period the woman looks after her
health and maintains sanitary standards in the home. Her
diet consists of only eating warm food. Although native
women do not have the finicality of the western woman,
they do take a series of precautions against miscarriage.
When the child is born the woman takes a bath known as
temaxcal which takes care of the after birth. In some communities activities very similar to those practised in the
prehispanic period take place, such as binding the umbili-
cal cord; if a girl is born, the cord is placed under the oven

with the ashes so that she will be able to make good tortillas and be a good house wife; if it is a boy the cord is buried in the field with a hoe so that he will be a good worker or farmer.

The seris use a portable cradle covered with pelican skin (Photo 188), the child is tied in, and the cradle hung from posts as they do in the south east of the U.S.A.

The child soon leaves his infant life behind and becomes integrated into the economic activities of the family and the community as a whole.

Social organization

There exist some institutions derived from the Spanish

(192) *In the Huastec area the new maize ceremony is held, in which tamales (a sort of maize pie) and atole (a drink made of corn mush) are cooked with the first maize of the harvest.*

(193) *As an offering to the calihuey or religious centre the Huicholes take cups decorated with glass beads. They also make bracelets with these beads.*

(194) *This is a comunal shrine of the Mazahua, in general the indigenous inhabitants mix prehispanic rites with Catholic beliefs.*

words such as "mayordomía" (stewardship) (Photo 189); in San Juan Chamula the person who had to be steward changed house and went to live in the ceremonial centre for one year; these people had considerable moral authority.

There are other posts such as "gobernadores" (governors), "alguaciles" (court officers), and others in which there is little difference between a political and a religious post, as both are occupied by the same person. (Photos 190 and 193).

Rarely is a woman able to assume these responsibilities.

Ceremonies

Among the most distant native groups are the Lacandones who have kept ceremonies like el Balche in which censers of a marked prehispanic style are used. (Photo 191).

The ceremony of the new maize is held in two native

(195) The majority of the Mexican indians share the custom of setting up an altar to the dead on the 1st of November as an offering to their relatives.

(196) Knowledge of herb medicine is a tradition which has been kept since prehispanic times.

day as children are always the first to be attended to anyway. In Patzcuaro, Michoacán, they light many candles so that the dead person will soon find his house and is not lost and "walking sorrowfully". Special bread for the dead is made at this time throughout the country and a special flower called the zempazuchil is cultivated.

Herb medicine

In Mexico at the present time there is still a large group of people who cure their ills by taking herbs, this comes from an old tradition of the quacks who made a profound study of the curative properties of plants (Photo 196).

(197) (198) Examples of Yaqui masks; the one with skin on the head is exclusive to the Chapayeca, a person who assumes power during Holy Week.

regions of Mexico, in Huastec and among the Lacandones; for this celebration they cook several plates of the first maize of the harvest. (Photo 192).

Among certain groups it is the custom to build and decorate small family shrines with pictures as these are used for private prayer; also people usually go to the main church in the community and to the mausoleum for the more formal ceremonies. (Photo 194).

The worship of the dead

A belief in another life existed in all native and mesoamerican groups, and underwent a change at the time of the conquest through the introduction of new ideas such as heaven, the devil, and others; but their basic concepts were not changed completely and the result was a mixture of both ideologies.

A very popular variation resulting from this mixture was the "altar of the Dead" (Photo 195) which is erected on the 1st and 2nd of November every year.

Relatives consider it obligatory to give an offering, as the dead person comes to eat and to spend these days with them; the offering consists of —brandy, maize pies, corn drink mush and clean clothes; if it is a woman, a loom and flowers are offered instead of brandy. Generally the dead are given water and some times money "for while they are looking for work".

The dead children receive their offerings early on the first

(199) Among the natives, masks have different meanings and uses.

Dances

The use of the mask is really universal, both in simple societies and in those of a more complex development (Photos 197, 198 & 199).

Nowadays the natives mainly use masks for their dances which are of several types according to the village and the type of festivity being commemorated. Some represent bearded Spaniards, old men, and devils; there are very few female ones.

Apparently, the most prehispanic of the masks depict animals such as the tiger and are used in dances reminiscent of ancient ritual.

The dances and ceremonies in general are accompanied by musical instruments, the ancient ones being the drums and flutes, but after colonization, guitars, violins and flageolets were introduced (Photo 200).

Among the dances that have been preserved for centuries is the so-called "venado" (the deer) of the yaqui; in this dance the lone dancer is adorned with "tenabaris" or butterfly buds on the wrists, ankles, and at the waist. (Photo 201).

In the Papantla area of Veracruz they still celebrate on Corpus Thursday of every year the ceremony of the "Volador" (flyer) dating from the prehispanic era and dedicated to the sun (Photo 202); in this dance five people climb a high tree, four come down and one remains aloft playing the flageolet. Those who come down do so head first and have to make 52 somersaults. There are several types of dance, one group called "conquest", among these, there is the Feather (Photo 203), the Malinche and yet others; it is interesting to note that in the speech accompanying the dance there are words in Arabic and old Spanish.

The three most typical dances of the Michoacán area are: the *Chinchilines,* the *Gualupita,* danced on the day of the feast of the virgin of Guadalupe, and perhaps the best known dance — *los Viejitos.*

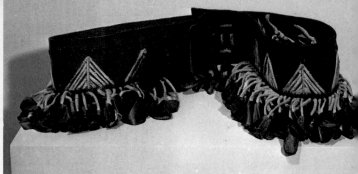

(200) Festivales and ceremonies are accompanied by music and dances. Percussion instruments, wind instruments of prehispanic type are used, also violins and guitars brought by the Spaniards.

(201) Perhaps one of the dances which has been kept unchanged since prehispanic times is the "venado" (deer) of the Yaqui in which the dance wears this belt with tenabaris.

(202) The ceremony of the "flyer" is typical of the Puebla mountains and Papantla in Veracruz; this is held on Corpus Christi Thursday.

(203) A dancer of La Pluma which is one of the dances known as "conquest".

(204) *The three typical dances of the Michoacan area are:
the Chinchilines, the Gualupita, in which a little girl dances,
and the dance of the Viejitos.*

Index

T.M. M.R.

Printed in Spain